BOA
EDITIONS LTD

Rue

Rue

Poems by

Kathryn Nuernberger

American Poets Continuum Series, No. 176

BOA Editions, Ltd. ⇒ Rochester, NY ⇐ 2020

First Edition
20 21 22 23 7 6 5 4 3 2 1

For information about permission to reuse any material from this book, please contact The Permissions
Company at www.permissionscompany.com or e-mail permdude@gmail.com.

Publications by BOA Editions, Ltd.—a not-for-profit corporation under section 501 (c) (3)
of the United States Internal Revenue Code—are made possible with funds from a variety
of sources, including public funds from the Literature Program of the National Endowment
for the Arts; the New York State Council on the Arts, a state agency; and the County
of Monroe, NY. Private funding sources include the Max and Marian Farash Charitable
Foundation; the Mary S. Mulligan Charitable Trust; the Rochester Area Community
Foundation; the Ames-Amzalak Memorial Trust in memory of Henry Ames, Semon Amzalak,
and Dan Amzalak; the LGBT Fund of Greater Rochester; and contributions from many
individuals nationwide. See Colophon on page 100 for special individual acknowledgments.

Cover Design: Sandy Knight
Cover Art: "Second Nature" by Elsa Mora Horberg
Interior Design and Composition: Richard Foerster
BOA Logo: Mirko

BOA Editions books are available electronically through BookShare, an online distributor offering Large-
Print, Braille, Multimedia Audio Book, and Dyslexic formats, as well as through e-readers that feature text
to speech capabilities.

Library of Congress Cataloging-in-Publication Data

Names: Nuernberger, Kathryn, author.
Title: Rue : poems / by Kathryn Nuernberger.
Description: First Edition. | Rochester, NY : BOA Editions, Ltd., 2020. |
  Series: American Poets Continuum series ; no. 176 | Summary: "Fiercely feminist ecopoetry exploring
  forgotten women naturalists, botanical birth control, and the ongoing cultural pressures women face in
  rural America"— Provided by publisher.
Identifiers: LCCN 2019036331 (print) | LCCN 2019036332 (ebook) | ISBN
  9781942683971 (paperback) | ISBN 9781942683988 (ebook)
Subjects: LCGFT: Poetry.
Classification: LCC PS3614.U85 R84 2020 (print) | LCC PS3614.U85 (ebook)
  | DDC 811/.6—dc23
LC record available at https://lccn.loc.gov/2019036331
LC ebook record available at https://lccn.loc.gov/2019036332

BOA Editions, Ltd.
250 North Goodman Street, Suite 306
Rochester, NY 14607
www.boaeditions.org
A. Poulin, Jr., Founder (1938–1996)

For Maya

Contents

>€

Rue

It's Like She Loves Us and Like She Hates Us

Our whole guise is like giving a sign to the world to think of us in a certain way but there's a point between what you want people to know about you and what you can't help people knowing about you.

—Diane Arbus

Sometimes I feel like that Diane Arbus portrait
of a woman with curlers in her hair and a cigarette
in her well-manicured hand staring too long
at the camera. Sometimes I feel like every character
I meet is an allegory of myself. John fell
from a ladder in his barn and broke his lawn mower
with his body but wasn't hurt himself at all.
It was so astonishing he's already posted about it
on Facebook three times. Reading between the lines,
you can tell he's worried maybe he actually died
in that fall. So I mess with him in the comments
and say something to that effect. He wonders if
there's a German word for this feeling. I tell him
there's a German exchange student crashing
at my house right now playing Hot Lava
with my kid. They call it lava in German too.
The German short "a" is so much like ours
it may as well be the same word. I'm worried
that John is really dead and the rest of us with him,
because there's no word for this feeling—
not even in German—and that's how you know.
I've been writing lecture notes this morning,
summarizing Plato's Cave for nineteen-year-olds
who will no doubt conclude getting a little high
is the way out. I assume this because that's what I did.
I have to remind myself I am not everybody.
Everybody in the cave is chained and suffering.
I have an animation to show them that retells the story
in clay, like a Gumby episode, except every still

frame echoes that government report on torture
released last month that is just one more example
of our denials as a society and complicity as a nation,
bolstered by the fact that photographic evidence
was censored and only later released through leaks.
I've read that torturers come to like their work and any
of us could, because we don't have a way to understand
another person's pain and we really want to understand
each other. My notes also include Susan Sontag,
who said fifty years ago in her essay on Plato
and photography, "Enough with the pictures already."
She was thinking of Dachau and thinking of Arbus.
The pictures, she said, feel like they're breaking
something inside ourselves we might have liked to keep.
I'd like to remember what picture I was looking at
when I was sober enough to realize there is no light
but this light. Maybe I just looked out the window,
as I did this morning, and saw my neighbor on his
mower, smoothing his lawn into that grassy plane
he likes so well. I felt a little closer to him, like he's
one of those portraits Sontag was talking about,
his face so hardened it's repelling at first, which is
why Sontag derides them so forcefully. I've found,
though, if you can make yourself hold on, all the faces
Diane Arbus made of people preparing to turn on
their show become so vulnerably human you start to fall
in love a little with the relentlessness of gazes. Even
the ones that are pathetic. Even the ones that are
pitiable. Even the ones that terrify for how much
they look like you. John, I think being dead suits me.

I'm Worried About You in the Only Language I Know How

There was a young woman with a boyfriend, I guess
that's what he was, on a bench beside her overstuffed
duffel bag. She was wiping at something in her eye
and when he motioned her to follow him and leave
the bag behind, she was slow to follow. He took her
by the hand and looking at her face, I was afraid for her
and also for us, sitting near this unattended luggage
as close as we were to the station, though I chastised
myself for being so bougie and anyway there she was,
just across the park, chatting with three men he
seemed to know, glancing now and again at her bag
like someone who'd be back in just a minute. We were
all in the shadow of a precarious metal sculpture
of two dragons interlaced with treacherous staircases
and slides for children. My daughter wanted me near her
on this wild ride, so then I was the one leaving our bags.
What is it in this upper class mothering experience
that makes it necessary to keep reminding myself people
hardly ever just steal your stuff? Every time I look
at this little girl of mine, I can't believe how much
I have to lose. Already I'd watched her take the plank
of the dragon's gleaming tongue so fast she slid
right across the pad onto the rough concrete and flipped
on her face. But she is tough, like a girl carrying a heavy
suitcase far from home, so she rubbed her raw cheek
and made a low growl to spit out the pain and went back up.
Once there was a hideout nestled in the interlocking tails,
but someone welded a cage door with a padlock
over the entrance. From the used toilet paper
that surrounds this place, I can understand why.
No one has taken that young woman's bag, I notice
from the crow's nest welded between a dragon's eyes,

but she is entirely gone now and so is that black van
the men were all leaning against. The one I thought
was her boyfriend is gone too. I'm worried about her
and all those backward glances. Because I've followed
men I shouldn't have trusted to places I didn't think
I could leave either. And even now I'm not sure
what I could have done differently. I tell my daughter
often that if you need help, look for a mother
with children. In a world of strangers, I can't imagine
the one who wouldn't try to help a child who asked.
Another kid is climbing up the slide. The first thing
she did was pull off her stockings so her bare feet
could give her purchase on the slick steel. She's
a clever little girl who knows where she is.
Whenever my daughter tries to lisp and stutter the bit
of language she knows here, other children stare
in silence as if her words have no meaning, so she
watches the big kid in mute admiration. And then
sets to work discovering what you can accomplish
with your own bare feet. I slip back to the bench
and pretend to look at other things, because I know
it's good for her to think her mother isn't always watching.
Beside my feet is that lost bag. I wish there were something
I could have thought to do about it. Something I had
known how to say when that girl caught my eye.

You Get What You Get and You Don't Throw a Fit

On the island at the other end of Whalefish-Upon-Leviathan
you'll find the people who are half man and half one huge foot
they use to hop around or umbrella themselves against the rain,
beast-women composed chiefly of fur and leaves, archers at war
with a battalion of blue cranes, and the conquistadors roasting
a headless man on a spit. It seems the world of fish goes on
into a forever of possibilities and then they wash up here,
on the beaches of Denmark, with their bellies full of squid
beaks and rubbery tentacles, their mouth-faces stretched out
into improbable grimaces, as if they swam straight from
the banks of that continent where the woman who was also
a bird has a body that is perhaps penguinoid, though you
wouldn't have thought until you saw this picture how much
the tuxedo belly of a penguin is shaped like a vagina waddling
around flip-flopping those awkward labia. She's bigger than
the men shooting their little arrows at her, it almost seems
they are the ones in danger, to study the crook of their smiles.
The fishmonger who wished his life had been something
different drew these maps of what he heard while he weighed
the sailors' hauls. Here's a star that blooms its six spiny legs
right out of the abyss of its own mouth. If you are generous,
you might call it a jellyfish. If you are generous, you can
almost make his illustrations match up to the world as you
know it. It is generous, after all, to draw one diagram after
another of everything you'd like to know. The lines of nations
and the swirls of ocean currents become true enough.
In each little demarcation of a city, the cartographer knew
of a man, he'd heard a story, they'd shared a drink. Each
of these sailors, their stars eternally etched at the mouth
of a river that cuts across the endless lavender of its country,
could be anywhere now. People disappear from this shore
into the bellies of fin-tailed monsters at an astonishing rate.

I wish I could imagine the roving stars of a woman or two,
but this is a story of the sea, not the biography of some girl
who thinks world history (1492–last week) should have had
a different x-y axis. The stars are in their places, the ports
in theirs. If there ever was one like me, she's plotted nowhere
except on a map of Latitude-What-Was and Longitude-
What-Might-Have-Been. Under such circumstances,
we must try to be generous with each other. It is
an extraordinary undertaking: Adriaen Coenen's 800-page
Visboek, commonly known as *The Fish Book*, contains
depictions of the no-less-than-seventeen-foot-long
sea beast who appeared off the Brazilian coast strutting
upon his hind flippers. It includes the zeebisschop with
his requisite hat, wand, slippers, chasuble, and gloves.
Of course, when I say "we must," I mean you must do
whatever you want and I will do the same. Sometimes
a very small god or a very small planet falls from the sky
and makes a splash. Sometimes a captain washes up on shore
and the world's largest, most cosmopolitan slave market
is born. I know you can't make a woman out of a boat
any more than you can find the mother you need in a penguin.
Adriaen left out the mermaids, as you must, if you wish
for your enterprise to be taken seriously as scholarship
and nonfiction. Mermaids, the cartographers have spoken.
Gather your cranes, brush out the leaves of your fur,
it is time we set sail, that we might be generous with
our plunder and generous with our spoils. That we might
star every city on this page with the lives we have known.

A Difficult Woman

I left the metaphor of myself I like best
in the rabbit warren and went to the office
to seem like the kind of person another person
might hire because it is a true fact that some
committee of persons hired me and this
because I pretended to be a Professionalism 4
once for an afternoon and that metaphor
was convincing enough to calcify over the flesh
of itself with a stiff-sleeved shirt and knee-length
skirt, and become the myself of myself now
who owes the office better than a Professionalism 3,
since the office is not the one who pretended
their way into this. The office is not the one
who didn't realize people really believe you are
how you pretend to be. The office is not
responsible for the fact I think curse words
bring flavor to any conversation and gossip
is a form of social capital essential to the building
of relationships because it makes a person
vulnerable and powerful with information
at the same time and forges a feeling, if not
the fact, of trust and authenticity. In pursuit
of Professionalism 4, I use a lot of smiley faces
and exclamation points in my discourse to iron
myself disarming. Professionalism 5 needs no
emoticons, for it is already ironed. I'm sorry
not sorry I left the metaphor of my uncomfortable
work clothes in the rabbit warren and decided
to wear jeans every day to every meeting
regardless of the pomp because no one asked
at the interview what I think about pomp.
I think pomp is maladaptive. That is

a Professionalism 2 sort of opinion to hold.
And anyway, I think pomp is fucking maladaptive.
I don't know why it is Professionalism 4
to keep that sort of opinion to ourselves.
I don't know why it is Professionalism 5
to love pomp. What if I fucking love pomp?
Would they have to create a box for 6?
Every little box is a warren and I try to stay inside,
but my haunches are itching springs and I want
to fuck over everything like it is May
and the oak leaves have just uncurled to the size
of squirrel ears. They billow more open, I think,
to try to hear the wind of all the discarded
metaphors for what I am and you are too.
The whole green lawn around the cinder block
of our days is buzz and bloom for somebody to,
I want to say *Kick up a tempest of themselves
getting fired*, but really I just mean *Tell me something
I don't already know and must swear never to repeat.*

I'll Show You Mine If You Show Me Yours

In the coffee shop was a guy with a really nice bald head
and one of those sleek jackets with the zip-up neck
that look great with a pair of well-cut jeans, which
he also had. I confess, I was looking him up and down
like a woman who has been reading Rumi and also a tome
on the history of bear cults in Europe. I just turned 35,
just got a promotion, just discovered the male gaze,
by which I mean I gaze on men like some sort of man,
by which I mean I'm hungry for my own hunger.
I'm like a mountain, I sometimes think, and I'm afraid
mountain is a symptom of menopause. When I became
a gourd blossom of pregnancy, I didn't know what
was coming. I died on that table and then woke up
to a nurse putting a swaddled baby in my wind-battered
petals. I won't be taken off guard twice. I know the time
is coming when I'll grow a mustache and my calyx
will turn to sandpaper. I'll be a volcano for a while,
then a crater, then a little sack of dusty bones. It makes me
fear-mad, like a man with a power tool and a tree
that won't come down. It makes me good at sex and good
at finding a guitar screaming in the interstices of the FM
dial of the big fat car I drive down the rumble strip
eyeing the men in hard hats on machines building a highway
out of molten tar just beyond the line of wind-quivering
orange cones. My man of this morning, I traced my eyes
right down his runner's leg to the modest woman's pump
he was wearing, black with a chunky heel and a Mary Jane strap.
Like I used to wear before I got this feeling I needed boots
with brown laces. I used to keep Mary Jane vows of silence
everywhere I went. Now, when someone I work with
is giving a presentation, I ask the follow-up questions.
Sometimes the question is halfway out before I even notice

I'm the one talking. This afternoon I heard myself saying
to the woman who had just finished clicking her way
through a PowerPoint, "You're doing great at being
professionally objective, but doesn't it ever just piss you off?"
The subject was the agency of heroines in Shakespeare's
comedies and her thesis was Chastity. When I'm a mother
in my own kitchen I tell my daughter, "You get what you
get and you don't throw a fit." By which I mean "Apples
and peanut butter." Poets I admire have been known to say,
"First thought, best thought." But if that worked I wouldn't
need to write at all. If that worked, I could just talk to people.
I wonder if Whitman ever walked out of some Manhattan pub
shaking his head at how hard it is to share a moment with
another human being. How you have to keep backing up
to explain yourself to your own fucking atoms. What I mean
is, I was reading an important tract on women's honor
and the critic (she's a philosopher but for some reason
we don't call her a philosopher) was lamenting how women
have historically been expected to lie, to cheat, to keep
their secrets. No one expects us to be honorable, only chaste.
I'm asking you if we can tell the truth in front of a room full
of people, and if that truth might not be that even Shakespeare,
especially Shakespeare, doesn't know us at all. And also
what I mean is, isn't it too bad we never really talk to each other.
Like, for example, about how I've been thinking about women
who have sex with horses. Because of Rumi's poem about
just that. Because of the bear cults too. Because I feel I might
be turning into a centaur. Because I feel I might want
to be turned into a centaur. Because the last thing I want
is to give birth to a centaur. Wasn't there a maiden
in the forest who couldn't keep her hands off the ears
of some enchanted donkey? Was it her chastity in the face
of his bestiality we admire? Personally, I'm partial to the way
she strains against such honor. Because I don't know
how to talk to people, I guess. Because I'm lonely.

I want to touch this man on the shoulder and say, "I like your shoes." But what I mean is, "I like what you are telling me with your shoes." Or what I mean is, "I like everything I know about you." But I don't say anything, because I think what I can hear you asking is if you can be allowed to pass unnoticed into the crowd of us. If that's what you want, of course. I won't say another word. I'll be quiet in my hope that I knew you as you wished to be known.

I Want to Learn How

Varieties of performance include:
        Being very nice. Or,
when you want to instead cultivate
a genuine friendship, you might be
very mean. Because who would perform
meanness? Or, as the old axiom goes,
true friends keep it real. But since
authenticity is a performance like
the rest, if you're still performing
either way, it's probably nicer
to play the part of nice, unless
your audience also longs for genuine
friendship, which most nice people do,
in which case you ought to be mean to them.
Except for the part where mean is mean.

Let's pause a moment and define our terms.

Nice = When Glen, a man I barely know
who frequents the only coffee shop
in this town, interrupts my quiet morning
with a book to ask about my garden
while he runs his hand across my shoulder
at first like some sort of greeting, but then
down my back, becoming bolder as I
become more stiff and distant. I do not
tell him this does not seem friendly at all,
but rather like an end-run around
social prohibitions against copping a feel
in public places on the bodies of women
you don't really know. He is one of the men
who owns this town, and I am a woman

who moved here but remains politically,
socially, and religiously outside of here. So I say,
nicely, "Tomorrow we're putting in okra."

Mean = When Glen, a retired police officer
I talk about gardening with at the coffee shop,
comes over to put his hand on my shoulder
and then my back, I stop him and say,
"Glen, it makes me uncomfortable
when you touch me like that. We're only
friendly acquaintances and that's a pretty
intimate gesture."

What to do = I can imagine Glen's sad face
when he realizes to his great embarrassment
that he's been one of those pathetic
old men touching and flirting with
a younger woman who was just being nice
but getting angrier each time. I don't like
that outcome. I don't want Glen to feel
he's been mean. It's not nice. I can also see
how Glen would, a few days or hours
later, when the sorry wears off, tell
the other men who run this town and sit
together every morning drinking coffee,
what a frigid bitch I am. He might phrase it
nicer than that, because he's a Christian man,
as he likes to say. But then I would see
the knowing eyes of those men everywhere
I go. Among the men at Glen's table
are the town doctor, who I may, someday
in an emergency, need to let touch me,
and also administrators from my workplace.
Sometimes I complain about how I can't
decide what to do about Glen to other men

who are friends of mine and with whom I also
work and who, at the office, outrank me,
but who also have children my child likes
to play with and wives I do not work with
whose husbands my friends at work
who outrank me have suggested I might like
to go shop with. I think these men might know
words I don't know for a situation like this
one with Glen because they are men
and perhaps this is a socially constructed
misunderstanding on my part. But no, they
agree it seems pretty sexual and inappropriate
and add that Glen probably knows pretty well
exactly what he's doing, as I suspected.
They shrug and say, "Why don't you just
tell him you don't like it?" Or they shrug
and say, "What's the big deal?" And I feel like
they have never really imagined themselves
inside such a situation and they don't really
think about how to imagine it even now,
when I am asking so nicely that they try. Why
are we even talking about something so small
and inconsequential, they seem to suggest
with their pinched tones and hunched shoulders.

Nice = Not talking about Glen any more.

Mean = Because I relive this coffee shop
dilemma 3+ times a week and it is the shop
where my friendship with these other men
unfolds too and because I like to work
and think in coffee shops and I like many
other people and talks I have in this shop,
the only one within thirty miles of my house
and place of work, and anyway should

we really solve the problem of harassment
in such a cowardly, impotent way, I say,
"Look, if we are really friends and if you don't
want to be another of these micro-aggressive
sexists perpetuating a patriarchal social system
through an attitude of dismissiveness
that makes it hard for some women to ever
feel comfortable being themselves or
saying what's on their minds, if that
kind of authenticity is even possible, you
should hear this story I'm telling as if it is
a serious conundrum of a moral nature.
Because it is not unreasonable for a woman
to think she has a responsibility to address
men crossing boundaries shamelessly
for the purposes of making a woman
into an object they feel free to touch, nor
is it unreasonable for that same woman
to worry that such correction in a town
this small will make it hard for her to continue
providing security and community
for her family in a town where there are
few jobs not at the chicken rendering facility
twenty miles south on Highway 39. And so
this small but unfixable situation will piss
her off and she will want to talk about how
she is pissed off, in no small part because
in general she is the kind of woman who
knows how to solve problems efficiently
with little fanfare and that is even one
of the reasons you hired her and like her,
if in fact you do like her."

What to do = I see these men who
have been friends of mine trying to arrange

their sad faces because they like to think
they themselves are feminists.
They'd tell a man not to touch them
in a heartbeat, they think, if it ever happened
to them. They'd tell Glen not to
touch me, if that's what I'm asking for.
It is not at all what I'm asking for.
If I were mean enough to decide
I really wanted us to understand
and know each other, as true friends do,
I don't know what I would say.
I might say all this. And then
they might say there are other words
besides *nice* and *mean*. They might say
there are other definitions. Perhaps they
will tell them to me, if I give them a reason.
Or perhaps they will walk away and we will
never speak of it again, as usually happens.

A Natural History of Columbine

When I met her she was playing her part
as the maiden who could not speak.
It was the Romantic Era, when mime
was still a sort of serious ballet, not yet
a circus act. Poor Columbine, always
being dragged by Harlequin from one side
of the stage to the other. This too because
it was an era when consent had not been
invented yet, so if she says yes or if she says
no, if she fights or if she succumbs—
these are not meaningful distinctions
for an audience so full of worries about
what will happen to them, regardless
of what they ask for. Columbine is a prop
the people have invested with strong
feelings of pity and concern. She is
a metaphor with a pretty body.

In this silent phase she could not say
whether she knew her name means dove,
a meaning she shares with the flower
whose blossoms hang in clusters like a cote
of birds brooding. She could not answer
whether her vow of silence came with
a vow of forgetting. Does she remember
how once upon a time a mother
or a midwife or an old witch at the edge
of town could give you a tincture of crushed
columbine in white wine to induce miscarriage?
Does she remember this is why she was
once known as the flower of unbridled
lust? That men crushed in their hands

her musk-scented seeds for courage
and virility? That lions ate her flower in spring
for strength? That the spur at the back
of the blossom looks as much like the talon
of an eagle as it does a slipper en pointe.

The good advice is always to know thyself.
As if any of us is walking around knowing
they are not knowing thyselves.

Columbine cries with her whole body
under the blue lights. She leans like a plant
on one toe after Pierrot, the lovelorn clown
in white who has neither the financial
wherewithal nor the violent disposition
to circumvent Harlequin's ambitions. But just
when you think there is no hope, a fairy
descends to swirl everyone off in a tempest
to the clouds where the dancing is more merry
and minor characters are turned into lobsters.

Then, intermission.

If you are studying the history of theater
and comedy, you might think of Columbine
as the granddaughter of Punch and Judy,
the famous medieval hand puppets.
Punch would hit Judy. Judy would hit
Punch. Sometimes they used bats.
The audience cheered and threw coins
in the hat. Columbine, the dancing beauty,
was there but not there, learning how funny
it was to see a man beat a woman bloody.
She tried to laugh along. Back then everyone
said Columbine blossoms looked like

jester hats so they called her the flower
of folly and foolishness and chuckled
to muss the little girl's hair when they passed
her, off at the side of the stage, waiting
for her folks to wash their faces clean
and set the dinner table. A day was coming
when she'd paint her forehead pale and rouge
her cheeks too. When she'd crimson her lips
into the pucker of two unfurling petals. The people,
always thinking they want something new,
would clamor for Harlequin's Columbine,
not Judy's Punch, even as they meant Judy's
Punch, not Pierrot's Columbine.

The years circle their tastes round and round.
Being myself more a Punch than a Columbine,
I say Pierrot would have done better to show
himself the affection he made into those relentless
invisible flowers with the dance of his silent
hands. His mooning about is so tedious.
And I suspect Harlequin wants nothing
more than the kiss of a stinging slap, though
I'm not so naïve as not to realize it might
be that he is another one of these who can
be satisfied by nothing but what he takes.

Oh this audience, with their handkerchiefs
to their eyes, as if this story represents
the meaning of their lives. You know
she's not even real, right? That she never was?
You can't be her, you can't be the clown
that had her. You can only be this scuttling
lobster the fairy won't change back, even now
that the curtain has fallen. Pierrot has bowed
with Columbine and Harlequin bowed

with Pierrot and Columbine dipped her curtsy
once more with the mayor and the magistrate
and the can-can girls, all these extras still
wearing their claws and boiled red leggings.

Lobsters can't talk either, though they can clap
after a fashion, so long as they have not
been rubber-banded and their clacking
is not lost beneath the roar of those crashing
waves. The meaning of their pantomime
is impenetrable and will come to replace
clowns and maidens as the archetypal figures
at the center of the Theater of the Absurd,
which is a kind of ballet and a kind of circus
that amuses the intelligentsia until it is
supplanted in another generation by
Artaud's theories of the Art of Cruelty,
when we watch a man shave his own eyeball
on the screen while dipping ourselves and others
in a rich butter sauce, with no idea how
it makes more sense than any of the gestures
that came before. Our mother, the flower,
our father, the joke, these are the stories we tell
our children over this glass of sparkling
white wine, letting them watch each little
bubble rise to the surface and pop, because,
as usual, we are at a loss for words as to why
we made some choices but not others, gave
ourselves over to this clown but not that one.

The Petty Politics of the Thing

I was surprised by the teeth and meat-breath
of myself. We're adults in an office. All the blue
computer screens hold very still and pretend
to be a beautiful view. It was not the kind of fight
a poem can understand, so I'll tell instead
about the cat who drug the newborn rabbit
from the nest under my porch. I'll tell you
that a bunny losing her throat screams like a panther
from within the fluff of herself. In a department
where everyone says they admire our collegiality
towards each other we file forms to chart
our feats of such-like professionalism. If
someone is testy another someone might
even say, "Thank goodness this is just a job
and we're not alley cats stalking a nest of rabbits."
And the vegetarian among us takes it hard,
because it's not collegial to ignore her sensitivities.
And the veteran among us who fought in a war
he can't talk about says under his breath,
"You think that's gruesome." But if anyone heard
him, they pretend not to. I don't know if it is
the cat in us or the rabbit that keeps so silent.
Sometimes in the course of a day I hear
the cat-rabbit in the back of my mind whisper,
"I will fuck you up." Oh, I love her. I love her
for how real she is. She can see through
even the most tangled bramble of rhetoric.
We are not animals, you learn over and over
in school, which is where they break you to
the fluorescent lights and geometry of so much
empty furniture in a room. Hush, little cat-rabbit,
I say. Thank you for reminding me, little cat-

rabbit, I say, it's enough just to know.
In that place I'm sad I'll have to die for a life
that was only ever a metaphor. I'll explain
to you what I mean as that little whisper
of a voice explained it to me. Money is
a symbol. Books are a symbol. The office
is a symbol. Your clothes may or may not be
a chain of severed heads around your neck.
Your diplomatic tone is the sharpened tip
of an obsidian stone. Don't feel mean,
I have one too. And when you say
I'm being melodramatic and not so much
is at stake in this silly bureaucracy
we idle our days through, little cat-rabbit
rumbles her stalking purr of *so-close now.*
To her, it is the very meaning of our lives
we squabble over and she's just been waiting
for someone to let me sink my teeth into it.

Pennyroyal

Pennyroyal, smallest of the mints, with weak prostrate stems.

Pennyroyal, a purple button for your pocket.

Pennyroyal, called Run-by-the-Ground.

Pennyroyal, called Lurk-in-the-Ditch.

Pennyroyal, "It creepeth much" and "groweth much." It comes into blossom "without any setting."

Pennyroyal, Pliny couldn't help himself going on at length.

Pennyroyal, creeping on my field for years.

Pennyroyal, before I knew what an old witch you really are, I brought you home to be a bouquet for my mother.

Pennyroyal, drunk with wine for venomous bites.

Applied to nostrils with vinegar to revive those who faint and swoon.

The inside of my body is very dark I think. Or maybe the skin lets a light in like when I close my eyes in the sun.

Pennyroyal, to relieve upset stomach.

Pennyroyal, to reduce flatulence.

Pennyroyal, active agent pulegone, I'll meet you in the centrifuge.

Pennyroyal, to flavor hog pudding with pepper and honey.

Strengthens the gums, helps the gout, cleanses the foul ulcers. Drives out the fleas.

Pennyroyal, for menstrual derangements.

Pennyroyal, to abort the thing.

Pennyroyal, to kill the bitch.

Pennyroyal, to take away the marks of bruises and blows about the eyes.

Pennyroyal, asked and answered.

"By putting flies and bees in warm ashes of pennyroyal, they shall recover life as by the space of an hour and be revived."

We're so many versions of ourselves. We try this, we try that.

Sometimes we're efficacious. Sometimes we don't know what we're for.

Poor Crow's Got Too Much Fight to Live

I'm watching an angry crow with his foot caught
in the chicken wire as his wings become his own
worst enemy. Poor bird, just lying there now breathing
his gasps of bottom ocean blue. Like when I was
giving birth I just got tired of giving birth after a while
and said forceps, suction, do with your knife, whatever.
Mercifully, the metaphors we have to live through
are fewer than the ones we think of. No one
is going to give birth anywhere near this crow
in the Dollar General parking lot. It would be easy
to free the bird from his situation, if he didn't
have so much fight left. When I told the doctor
after 68 hours, "Yes, to anything. Do whatever
you think is best," he took a huge suction cup
and pushed it all the way through me to the baby's
head and had a nurse squeeze the pressure gauge
as he tugged my child out of my body's confused grasp.
I watched him sweat and grimace his pulls just right.
You could see it was hard what he was doing for me
and I felt so sorry about that for months. A woman
isn't supposed to be grateful to a man for birthing
the baby for her. That's the patriarchy I wanted to push
out of, but I was so grateful to him I could almost forget
about the inherent sexism in our every system,
including the medical industry. I could even almost
forget about the other doctor in his practice I saw just once
while my good, dear doctor was on vacation. That guy
jammed his hand into me hard and without warning,
I think because he was offended by our conversation
about my birth plan, which was boilerplate stuff
about avoiding drugs and letting my body run its course.
I'd like to prosecute him, for myself and even more

for everyone else, but it took me months to understand
what he had done and why and by then it could so easily
be time telling the story instead of truth. I mean,
let's look at the uncertainty of facts: He and I talked
about the natural birth plan that I had shared previously
with my regular doctor, because it was sitting there
in my file and he asked. I interpreted his face
during that conversation as annoyed. I interpreted myself
as meek because I was not wearing pants and you could see
the shadow of my pubic hair through my paper blanket.
I nodded along noncommittally to the things he said.
My real doctor would be back soon enough. He told me
to put my legs in the stirrups. Normally a doctor will
adjust my thighs and say something like "you're going to feel
a touch" and that's when I exhale, but his hand was already
in me, I was startled and uncomfortable, and his nurse
who follows him from room to room was at my ear so quick
saying in a nurturing voice, "Practice your breathing dear,"
as if this normally happens, but also as if there was
some kind of emergency. It was taking a long time
and hurting a lot, the nurse's talking about breathing
really made me frightened. I was worried something
was happening to the baby, I couldn't even see the doctor
over the mountain of my pregnant belly. Then he said,
"If you do this while you're in labor I won't be able
to help you." I couldn't tell what "this" I was doing
besides waiting for him to stop what he was doing.
Time has helped me hear those words as a threat
of punishment for disregarding his authority,
as I think they were intended. Or maybe it is true
that I tightened the muscles in my vagina in such a way
that he couldn't get his hand out and I was crushing him.
Maybe it is true that can happen? I should ask a gynecologist.
Do you know one who will talk about sexual assaults
committed by other members of his or her profession?

I haven't met such a doctor yet. When I was pregnant
for the first time a different OB gave me a pap smear,
and that was also uncomfortable, as you would expect,
but then she was the one startled and nervous
and telling the nurse there was a lot of blood and asking
for a cauterizer and asking me if I had a tipped uterus.
I said I didn't know what that was, so she carried on,
cauterizing something at the far end of my vaginal canal
near what I would call my tipped uterus until another OB
would tell me all uteruses are tipped, so that was
a weird thing for her to say. When the bleeding stopped
she sent me for an ultrasound. The baby was fine,
robust heartbeat, little beautiful fish we watched swim
with the very beginnings of her arms and legs,
but a few weeks later I miscarried anyway, and the doctor
never said her hand slipped nor did she say I suddenly
clamped down. She didn't say anything except
that these things sometimes happen. And they do.
I knew most likely she was telling the truth and I knew
she wouldn't tell if it wasn't. Whatever the reason,
I don't blame her, but I'd like to know what's true
about the other one. I'd like to file a police report,
in case there are other women like me, because
of course there are other women like me,
but it's been five years, I live in a different state
now, and I'm not even sure I believe myself.
Even after the unexpected phone call from a nurse
who gave no name, her subtle questions, I'm not sure.
I'm sorry, other people he might have or still yet
hurt, but I'm not so naïvely idealistic as to think
any good could come of saying to the public that I was
assaulted by an OB/GYN in his office in Logan, OH
in May 2010 and I'm willing to testify to that.

I Want to Know You All

I was listening to this sort of ignorant blowhard
go on about how teaching is a dumb profession
and I did this thing I always do, which is feel smug
about how smart and sophisticated I am, but
my smugness is a little compromised lately
by how I do almost nothing all day besides have
an affair in my mind and then wring my brain
over what a divorce would do to my daughter,
who heretofore has been lucky to have a happy,
close family, not even too far off from how we
pretend to be in public. So I just kept listening
without my hackles up so much and also was
bemused about how alike we all are, admiring
some people, judging others, thinking we're so
special, and this guy had some good stories.
One time a history professor in college told him
to go hang himself after he wrote 500 words
about pheasants in the French Revolution.
He said he must have mentioned those fired up
and pitchfork-wielding pheasants a dozen times
in that paper. That exasperated historian screaming
PEASANTS in the margins always reminded him
of his dad, who does probate, which is basically
a ton of archival research into plat maps and deeds,
birth certificates and death wishes. There are no
secrets when someone contests a will. His dad
once told him, "You wouldn't believe the number
of cross-dressing farmers there are in Missouri,"
which made me laugh at first at the hypocrisy
of this place, but then realize it's actually tragic
how alone those farmers must feel. It's ruthless
out here, I know. All the longing we till under

only to let such a secret slip—probate means some
cousin or sister or brother described the dress
in front of a judge who considered it fit evidence
against a claim. I laughed because I can't imagine
who you are—the man in coveralls who mocks
the foamy fern I like poured onto my latte,
the one who calls me "hon" that condescending
way? Or are you the one always with the sign
in front of my doctor's office or the neighbor
who mows the waysides of our country road
down to stubble? Maybe you don't come to town
if you can help it anymore either. I want you
to know, whoever you are, as someone hungry
for variety in the human condition, most especially
my own, cross-dressing farmers, you light up
the fields for me. I hope you walk into those
soybean rows some nights and your flowered skirt
swishes your legs in a way that feels like falling
in love when you didn't think you ever could.
Or maybe you feel rooted, belonging to this soil
that made you. I don't know what's better, but
I want for you such happiness and every last acre
your bigot of a father left behind to go with it.

Paradise by the Dashboard Light

When I think of what I know about you
I think of the way mirrors in a dressing room
can do that trick with each other
that makes a single person go on forever.
I think of a private hole in the ground
where a kid drops an acorn and we don't
expect to ever see it again. I think of how
I should see a therapist. Or maybe
get a CT scan, in case this feeling isn't
a feeling, because really, it's excessive,
don't you think? I think of what I know
about you, which is to say, I think about
how small a day is and then I count them
on my fingers. Then I count down the years
to menopause while I'm at it. Then
I think about what it was like to be sixteen,
that stupid prom dress with the purple
sequins, not unlike the wedding dress
I grabbed off the rack because a costume
is a costume. I'm thinking about you
when I hear one of those rock anthems
on the electric guitar with the lyrics
about how great and tragic it is
to have sex in the back of a car and I
almost run my sedan with the empty
booster seat in back off the highway
I'm laughing and crying so hard at what
it was like to be a virgin dancing
to that song and when I think of what I know
about you, I remember my best friend,
Amanda, under a strobe light shaking
her booty like someone who knows how

to be happy, then motioning with her finger
to get me on the dance floor. And sure,
I'm the kind of girl whose legs don't work
right when it comes to getting off the bleachers—
I don't think that has changed—but I love
watching her grab her boyfriend by the tie
in a cheesy choreographed way
and sing the words straight into his face
as loud as she can. "Will you make me
so happy for the rest of my life?
Will you take me away? Will you
make me your wife?" I think I love
growing up and knowing I'll never again
have to pretend to be sixteen and then I think
about how a sixteen-year-old would have
kissed you all night long and then
written a very silly song about it.
She would have believed all the words.

When We Dead Awaken

When you look at a long wave of kelp stretched out
as it if were a mess of some drowned girl's hair, you won't
be thinking of the functionality of the ovoid bladders
like tiny buoys holding the flat wide blades towards
the sun for maximally efficient photosynthesis.
You'll be thinking of that time you almost reached
to hold the hand of a man as he told you that story
where two teenagers don't fuck on the beach, but do
find the corpse of a pregnant girl washed up on the sand.

The wind on the bluffs of everything we didn't
do felt crisp and clear, but down below on the gray beach
sand fleas would swarm you as you walked among dumps
of seaweed and shore-battered crab husks. I know
because I walked the lip of it alone at the end of this.

If you feel like you're in love, you have to either remember
or forget that a feeling can only last a little while.
What you should do with your little while, I can't say.
The history of should is the history of honorable men
discovering Caribbean beaches with white sand and water
as blue as a mermaid's eyes, where they dragged human beings
down the gangplank in chains to finance the invention
of coffee shops and decorative buttons on ladies' shoes.

The coast I have in mind was so ashen and the pines were
brown with the fire-drought of the end of our present world.
I should have taken his hand. I've already been a pregnant girl
washed up on shore twice. The bull kelp are so big I thought
I was looking at a dead squid the first time I saw one. I asked
the shoulder of him I wanted to lean my head against if he
thought that was even possible. He said anything is possible.

You don't understand how long it was I had been dead
by that night of the day Maya took me to her lake at the edge
of the peninsula daggering this gray sea. It is a lake so old
a glacier carved it right down to the bottom of the basalt earth.
When you jump in—and you have to jump in—the cold
stops your heart for a second and then it comes back
in a seizure of beating that makes your vision blur.
That is also a feeling that can only last so long.

A boyfriend threw his dead girlfriend in Maya's lake once
and the mineral waters iced over that night. When spring came
nine months later, the fishermen found her floating in the water
as perfectly beautiful as when she went in. They call her Lady
of the Lake and she haunts the place as a ghost or a witch
or a very old god who still remembers how to want and how
to grasp what she wants with the ice of her hungry fist.

It was night. I couldn't get the stars to hold still. I couldn't
catch my breath. I was 1000 miles outside of my life. How long
since I felt anything? And now there was nothing
I could not feel. I could see beyond the sails and red lights
of the coast guard buoys, the flashing tentacles of a hundred
squid rising up to taste the silver of that strange moon
before the surf hurled them in lumps at our feet.

I have a dead daughter I carry like a smell of salt spray
in my mind and I have an alive daughter who is home running
with her kite straight into the wind. I have but also
do not have the rest of you. I don't see how we can be
longer than a story to each other. It's not me. It's the waves.
My arms are so tired, I just need to float for a while.

There was no squid. It was a wrack of seaweed bulbs,
their squish stems wrapping in each other, strange creatures,
soft as leaf, firm as fish, forming of themselves a forest

against the physics of diffusion and drift. If I had that night
back, I'd do it wilder this time. Not like the silent mist
of a ghost maiden, but like a red-eyed revenant who has
figured out at last how to reach across the veil of breakers
and grab the girl of some dying woman by the heart
and make her beat until she's gasping once more.

Whale-Mouse

When we fall in love, if we fall in love,
we do it alone. But it is not enough
to be the only person in love
with Carl Linnaeus, who invented
the *Systema Naturae* we use even to this day
to classify all living things, who named
the flowers Latinate translations
of "little frog" or "little nymph."
I need you to love him too. For how
every genus, every species becomes
a metaphor for some other genus or species
until the flowers are toads and the toads
are fish and the fish are the flowers
of all those constellated deities zodiacing
our sky. He named one bloom of a thing
after himself and pressed *Linnea borealis*
in the sketchbook he carried with him
everywhere so he would never forget an idea
or a moment that made him wonder.

In this century I knew a man
who did the same. It broke open
a mollusk in my chest every time
he scribbled some inconsequential thing
I said into his little book to keep.

Have I mentioned Carl Linnaeus was
the one who put a piece of limestone
deep into the mouth of a mollusk
and cultivated the first artificial pearl?
It's all so personal and private, these
notebooks, how he drew Andromeda

as a child might, naked and out of
proportion, standing in an open clam.
She is being threatened by a newtish
sea monster. Beside her like a sister,
the plant he named *Andromeda* towers
over an actual newt who cowers beneath
the curved spine of her stem. He made
hundreds of these sweet jokes in his
intimidating tomes. *Mus musculus,*
for example, is "little mouse." Blue whale,
largest being in the sea, who must rise
to breathe our air, as mammals do,
perplexing and tangling categories
for years, he named *Balaenoptera musculus,*
or "the mouse whale." I can't carry a feeling
this heavy and beautiful for someone
by myself. I have to give it to you.

He was a man in trousers and a wig
in the 1700s, but paid such attention
and care to everyone he met that he knew
to name the butterfly pea *Clitoria.*
He took that notebook on an expedition
to Lapland where he drew an owlet
and a bundled baby. He made notes
while the women explained how to cure
chilblains with roasted reindeer cheese
and fix a broken pot by boiling it in milk.
He asked the men to teach him to make
thread from the reindeer's hooves.
On another page he chronicled the bold
endeavor undertaken with his dear friend
George to grow the first banana
in Europe. In faint pencil beneath
a careful and detailed portrait of the fruit

they nurtured together through the winter,
he asks, "Will it grow for years?"
Though it was his ambition to know
everything and name it all, he was
humble enough to be certain he wouldn't.
When unsure which genus an animal
belonged to, he put it in a box labeled
"worms" for further investigation
some other time when his own worm
of a brain might be ready to solve
the puzzle of its being. When unsure
whether an animal was real, it went
in the column "Paradoxa." His was a time
of unlimited possibilities. Dragons,
unicorns, pelicans—all were "Paradoxa."

There is much in this life that is not
what it seems. There are moments—
in Lapland, perhaps, or some other
far corner of this earth, beside a fire
beneath a northern sky full of stars—
that cannot last longer than a night.
Moments when some extraordinary
person reaches across the grass
that separates you to hook just one
of his fingers around just one of yours.

The day will come when a better
historian than I tells me how Linnaeus
also classified people into columns
of white, black, yellow, and red. It will
break the mind of my heart and I won't
understand how it can be that even he
was just another man, nothing more
and maybe even something less than

that small pink flower of his most perfect
name I once loved to say. What do you
think? Can we love him anyway? Did we
ever really even in the first place?

The Bird of Paradise

Out my window I have a little city lawn that slopes
down to the asphalt. The single drop of dew bending
the bulb of a wild onion reminds me of The Old Man
Who Asked Why. He hung onto his perch of steeple
at the top of the moon, unflinching, refusing to say
anything but "Why?" He was visited by the Angel
of Other People's Troubles, who grew so angry
and tired of this that he threw The Old Man Who Asked
Why down from his steeple on the moon all the way
to the earth. As he fell he grew younger and younger
until he was a young man, a teenager, a boy, a baby,
touching the ground softly just in time to be born.

I'm making a little notebook of pressed flowers
with my daughter. We learn their names in Latin
and we learn the names the midwife-witches
would have used. If they are safe to eat, we eat
them; we brew them and dry them and salve them.
It is a way to know them and a way to know
ourselves as creatures among them.

There was a kind of peacock flower Maria Sybilla
Merian drew flawlessly, its stamen uncurls like
a luxurious tongue licking butterflies right out
of the air. The yellow cheeks of petals buttercup
their way around the seductions of vines.
The rich depth of those seeds—crushed
they make the richest black ink in the world.

It was the kind of ink John Stedman might have used
to record the sights that greeted him when he
stepped onto the country of that flower's far shore.

In his notebook he wrote his first impressions
of the Dutch colony of Surinam:

            "A revolted negro hung alive on a gibbet
with an iron hook stuck through his ribs,
            two others chained to stakes and burned
to death by slow fire,
            six women broken alive on the rack,
            two girls decapitated . . ."

Maria Sibylla Merian, the great woman botanist
and first ecologist, having escaped her marriage
and then her country, returned home from Surinam
with an indigenous woman. She brought also
such treasures as frog eggs in jars of brandy
and butterflies pressed between the pages of a book.
Trunks of chrysalises and snakeskins and other
botanical specimens were a kind of hedge fund
a divorcée naturalist could leverage to the fashionable
armchair collectors of Frankfurt. She said in letters
that she had suffered fever and disappointment.
Though likely she was not so disappointed as she
might have been, being still upper-class and European
in the Age of Empire. Would she have imagined
this other woman to be her friend or her property?

No matter how long I linger over
the botanical textbooks, I can't figure out
the difference between monocots and dicots.
We pull apart the old tulip, take scissors
to the part where the pedicel meets
the ovary. I'm wondering if we might
be able to see the ovule. Instead we find
an ichorous mess of pale, hardening green.

"The Indians, who are not treated well by their
Dutch masters, use the seeds to abort their children,
so that their children will not become slaves
like they are. The black slaves from Guinea
and Angola have demanded to be well treated,
threatening to refuse to have children. They told me
this themselves," Maria Sibylla Merian wrote
in her footnote to the portrait of that beautiful flower.
She does not name her source for this knowledge.

Maria Merian's first book was about caterpillars.
She was a most unusual artist and a most unusual
scientist for how she painted insects on their host
plants. Because her plants were always surrounded
by their pollinators, she is called the first ecologist.
Even as a girl who had been given a present
of a silkworm, it was dangerous and must be kept
secret, this interest in things that creep and crawl
and grub. Before she discovered metamorphosis,
it was thought the flying things spontaneously
generated or were tormentors sent up from Hell.
She had to be cautious with her propriety—
butterflies were still believed by many to be
transfigurated witches doing the devil's work
to sour the milk. It was the end of one mean age,
everyone so hungry or afraid of being hungry
again, and the beginning of another; she would
have been foolish to think herself safe from
the accusations of those who feared witches, those
who feared women, and those who feared science.

I like the defiance of the plants. They are
at odds with themselves—they do one thing
and also do its exact opposite. You can treat
the burn of stinging nettle with a compress

of stinging nettle. One dose of a plant
will save a life and another will end it.
With tweezers and a microscope you can see
how any bouquet is a collection of revolutions.

Before she set sail for the islands, she was cautioned
and cautioned again that white women in warm
climates succumbed "to copious menstruation,
which almost always ends, in a short space of time,
in a fatal hemorrhage of the uterus." Also that
"the intense African sun" will produce "black babies,
regardless of the mother's complexion."
These admonitions were of no concern to her.

To escape her husband she joined a religious sect,
the Labadists. They had a vision of a world filled
with daughter communities, of which Providence
Plantation in Surinam was one. There is a saying
about how the day comes when it is more painful
to a bud to hold onto its flower than it is to open.

But what to make of the letters home?

          "The wild ones are hostile as tapirs."
          "The heat is so extreme we cannot work."
          "Here no one thinks or speaks of anything
that is not sugar cane."
          "The slaves refuse to work when the saints
are so good to them, so we must resort to the same
beatings and blows used by the fallen."

The slaves who survived had their accounts too:

          "In slavery there was hardly anything to eat."
          "It was at the place called Providence Plantation."

"They whipped you there until your ass was burning."

The Merian family crest Maria had printed on frontispieces
of each of her books was a stork holding a snake in its beak.
An echo of the Madonna crushing the serpent beneath her
bare feet, it is meant to be a symbol of justice and piety.

She didn't know much Latin. Women had no occasion
to learn it. She used instead the names the indigenous
people used and footnoted each flower with the uses
the indigenous people knew. She had the idea a plant
was not an object you picked out of the field, but a point
of intersection for pollinators and predators and fruit
and weather. She might have extended this ecology
even further to include the human societies that grew
up around them. Perhaps she did. She left the plantation
saying she had grown ill. She left the Labadists too.

In 1647 in every ditch and byway of Europe there were
plants growing that you could have used to prune back
the abundance of your body, but you'd have had to catch
a witch-in-butterfly to get the recipe. In the footnotes
to a book of pretty flower engravings this woman's secret,
revealed in such plain terms, is very great and dangerous.

The post-colonialist historians are wise to ask
what Maria Merian thought the landed gentry
who bought her books would do with such information
they paid her so well to receive. Open an apothecary
for women like her, revolutionaries of independent means?
More likely they would have cleared their property lines
of such plants that might reduce the propagation
of their investment in human capital. There is a point
at which giving so much benefit of the doubt becomes
another exploitation and the conditional tense

just a grammar for the naïve or the lying. Maria Sibylla
Merian was many things, and included among them
is the fact that she could be self-serving and cruel.

A woman with no name and no story is holding out
a flower. I don't know this woman. I have tried to imagine
her. I have tried to imagine being her. To be human,
after all, is to look at each other and imagine how
it would be. But then again, maybe we are not
so capable of everything we imagine ourselves to be.

It could have been any of us, but it was her
who lived her life, her who died that life,
her whose name the botanist never once
bothered to write down in a footnote
or journal or dashed-off letter. Most likely
it was her secrets so carelessly given away.

That seed makes the darkest ink
a blank page has ever swallowed.

There is an old man who will not stop asking
why. Our ears will not stop ringing with it.
There is an answer that is a silence that grows
longer and deeper as you peer into it.

It is one of the most vibrant blossoms
to spring out of this earth—
its crimson tongue, the ocher of its petals.

Dear Reader, I've Been Preoccupied Lately by My Own Private Business

I was supposed to be telling you about this silly collection
of past-futuristic philosophers who went to the moon
in a movie in 1902, back when philosophers couldn't talk yet,
so they had to point at their chalkboards with greater
or less than enthusiastic intellectual exuberance before
piling into a rocket ship as if it were a clown car.

Back when we were all sitting in that starry house of a swan
under Venus's flickering light I couldn't stop feeling
like too many eager aeronauts were clambering in me.

I don't know what changed to make me into this rock with no atmosphere.

Although of course I know exactly what changed.

I just don't want to talk about marriage right now.

Their moon, when they got there, was full of can-can girls.
Their moon wanted a fist in the kisser.
Their moon wanted to pull off those stockings.
Their moon was orbited by a comet made of fire, not some accuracy of ice.

It was all so close to the night that the face of sky
and our faceless rock breathed moist stratosphere
on each other like the earth and the sea
primogenerating themselves. If I try I can still
at least talk myself into feeling like a celestial event.
I take a minute here and there throughout the day
to set my poor asteroid spinning with the memory.
What I can't do is make myself forget it's a trick.

Over the course of a hundred years, how can a person help but learn
to look for the wires, the line where the mask reaches the ears,
the black-winged fluttering of a stop animation?

Ask the philosophers about what can be helped.

There were constables and presidents trying to push them
off the launch pad of their folly. You wouldn't expect old men
with white beards to fight and bite and kick with such vigor.
That's what makes it all so very funny.

I see you down there.
All your passions and your dramas.
The vitality of your tangled velvet cloaks.
I see how charming it is to dream in color while you live in black and white.

Once, it would have been enough to make me laugh out loud.

Do you think the stars are better if you're standing
on some precipice of moon? I don't know, because
in all the movies the first thing they do is turn
their telescope full of eye straight for home, as if
the chance to look back was the only reason they left.

Queen of Barren, Queen of Mean, Queen of Laced with Ire

If a woman dreams of lace, it is said,
she will be happy in the realization
of her most ambitious desires
and lovers will bow to her edicts.

There were two Annes—the one who dreamed of lace
and the one who dreamed of waxen seals, as there are two
Queen Anne's Laces—the one with the purple dot at its center
like a needle prick of spilled blood, which is edible wild carrot,
and the one with no dot, stalk spackled in purple like Socrates'
blood, it is said, though he spilled no blood when he was
executed by hemlock, which is non-edible wild carrot
also blooming in an upturned face of white blossoms.

Carrots, it was said, are such an aphrodisiac Caligula amused himself
by feeding the court nothing but, then watched them rut like animals.

When I lived in that lonely place, I bought a field guide to learn the name
of every flower. There were not many to learn, stitched as I was to a field
between a cascade of crop-dusted corn on the left and an ocean of soy
on the right. Where there might have been poppies and cornflowers
and honey bees needle-pointing the rows, only Queen Anne's Lace
was hardy enough to make a kingdom out of such long-barren dirt.

My ire at these impossible, 7-dusted acres.

My ire at the billboards with ultrasounds as big
as a cloud floating over the rows of copyrighted
beans, irrigated so green.

When everything on a tract is alive and buzzing, a fallow field
will bloom one medicine after another. If you look them up

in Culpeper's guide or Pliny's, almost all in leaf or seed or stem,
some small dose or a large one, will "provoke the menses,"
as the euphemism goes. When everything is alive, there is never
a week when the soil does not offer you some kind of choice.

When I lived in that lonely place I thought I'd turn to
Rousseau, who understood so well what we give up
in exchange for the social contract, who wrote the great
treatises on romanticism and democracy from his place
in exile. Rousseau, I thought, my antidote to this minister
who does his abstinence-only counseling for teenage
girls and pep talks the boys on Godly masculinity just
one dinner table over. If you knew how many times
I've heard, "Our Lord is a jealous lover."

But he is also Rousseau who dumped his bastard children
in an orphanage. Rousseau who had no care for what
the social contract did to the women he took as lovers
and then left as lovers. Rousseau who goes on and on
about breastfeeding and natural motherhood like a man
who has no idea. Had Rousseau written his botanical letters
to me, his "dear and patient lady," with the tedious thought
experiment of teaching a "most willing pupil" to visualize
the flowers through written language alone—"After you have
looked over my letter once or twice, an umbellate plant
in flower will not escape you"—I would have been too eager
to agree with his postscript. "The meanest kitchen-maid
will know more of this matter than we with all our learning."

In describing the umbellate Queen Anne's Lace in flower,
a maid would not have forgotten to mention that crimson
dot at the center calling the braconid wasp to his favorite
pollenatrix. This drop, it is said, the queen pricked from
her own finger on the spindle of her perfect lace. A drop
that slips from a kitchen-maid when the great philosopher

returns from the prairie of his letters to the greener pasture
of her idealized womanhood. A maid would not have forgotten
the mark by which she knows which umbelliferous queen stops
your heart and which one sets it beating once more.

It is said the queens upset the cows' milk if they founder
on too much lace. It is said the queens upset the sheep's
digestion, but watch the hoofed beasts and see how they know
after a miscarriage to graze the medicine of those leaves.

At the end of the season the blossoms turn brown and brittle
and close in on themselves like a bird's nest. The meanest
maid knows this is when you gather your clumps of seeds.
No one writes down what the kitchen-maids say, so no one
is anymore sure whether you drink them only after sex
or every day or when you are ovulating or for the full
two weeks between ovulation and menstruation. Some say
you must chew the seeds to release the tannins. Some say
drink them down in a glass of water. Some say it is a crime
to publish such information. Some say only that it is a liability.
Now in the laboratories of the minds of the great thinkers
they call it rumors and old wives tales. As if none of us
has ever needed an old wife. As if only fools would
allow themselves to turn into such wizened things.

There was Anne I who was known for making beautiful lace.
And there was Anne II who was known for her sixteen
miscarriages, four dead children, and slipshod petticoat
of a government. There was Anne I who employed subterfuge
and intrigue to manipulate the king's policies. And there was
Anne II who had no king and no heir and no wars and hardly
even an account of discontent among the flourishing and well-fed
people. And yet what is said of her is only that she was Anne
the fat, Anne the constantly pregnant, Anne the end of her line.

My ire at the kingdom.

My ire at the kings.

My ire at the philosophers who think
they can just reinvent the world
inside the eye of their own minds.

What I want I want on terms as I dictate them.

My ire at my terms.

My ire at my impossible wanting.

That I can be no flower and be no field, my ire.

That there will be more castrated queens,
an endlace necklace of almost enough, my ire.

My ire, if you wait enough years, the field will finally grow.

If you wait years enough you will be long dead, my ire.

Things I Did Today Besides

I looked at mulberry paper diagrams of a woman's brain
made by the artist Lisa Nilsson, who says this rolling
of the gilded spines of old books into something else
was a practice designed by Renaissance nuns and monks
making artistic use of scraps, later perfected by eighteenth-century
ladies making artistic use of a lot of free time. I was
impressed. Then I read some love poems by a famous
writer who does an excellent job controlling himself.
I was not impressed. I also read something by my friend
who is not yet a famous writer, who is also controlling
herself, but just barely. She and I feel so many of the same
things that we only communicate them via poems. Part
of what we have in common is that we'd never talk about
an affair out loud, much less have one. Unless one of us
actually has one. If it has to be one of us, I hope it is me.
I have too long been so excellent at controlling myself.
But my chance to make a gilded wreck of everything
is getting moth eaten by the absence of a new letter
from the only person who has ever made such a pulp
seem possible. I knew when I didn't leave my husband
right that minute I would come to think I was crazy
to have thought I wanted to. Which was the worst part
of not doing it. And now here I am, looking on the past
with the serene composure of a woman learning to like
her compromises. In Book 3, Chapter 9 of his *Travels*,
Marco Polo mistook a rhinoceros for a unicorn because
he believed what he read in books. You can't fault
him for that. You might even think, *What does it matter
if you call a unicorn a rhinoceros or vice versa? They're just words.*
But if you think that, you too are desperately in need
of a very well-written letter that reminds you of the words
for everything you don't know. Before all of this,

in the matte light of morning, I rolled over and put my
head on my husband's chest and told him, *I still want
to revenge kiss a stranger.* Even though I don't really want to,
I want to, so I'm making myself want to. Telling him this,
I said, was a gift. A gold-leafed box of dramatic and secret
and honest. It's everything I want from a relationship
and I'm giving it to you. When he kissed my temple
and said *I know*, I knew it was possible to be moved
by the love story of this sort of thing that leafs between us.
But I'm no longer satisfied by such pages. I'm consumed
with what a nun can do with a busted-up spine. It's called
quilling, by the way, and it requires a great deal of intense
concentration. So much, in fact, it wouldn't be at all
surprising for a virgin to suddenly feel she saw the erotic
face of God in the work of her slender, efficient fingers.
I could envy her the finely-etched mulberry branches
lacing this box of pleasure she found in her otherwise gray
convent of a life, but I do not. I've changed my mind
about the whole thing. How stupid must you be to not
know that pretty boxes are a dime a dozen? You can fill
your whole house with them, if that's what you want.

The Threshold of the Unseen World

I'd like to propose that Anna Atkins and Alexander von Humboldt
were meant to be together in a great love affair that would prove
the existence of God to anyone within a hundred years of their
thermodynamic union. That they never met, never wrote a letter,
never received one, never lived in the same place in the same
century, never traced a finger down the spine of the other's book
means I may as well be in love with Anna or Alexander myself
for all the good a feeling means. Which is a relief of a conclusion
since I have this soggy heart full of India ink and no one will take
that cup. In *On the Threshold of the Unseen* William Barrett wrote that
"it is not a very incredible thing to suppose that in the luminiferous
ether . . . life of some kind exists." Daimonia, some physicists
called them, others said elementals, later we'll say particles. "Could it
not be that life itself is a peculiarity handed over from the invisible
to the visible?" Alexander took a cyanometer with him on his voyage
to measure the color of sky against his wheel of impossible
gradations, a hopeless blue that promises there is no true blue,
only the place where we sit down halfway up the mountain
and say this is blue enough for me. But Humboldt never once
sat down. He recorded 23.5 at noon overhead drifting through
the still waters of the Caribbean, 41 at the summit of Teide
in the Canary Islands, 46 when the cloud cover broke over the ledge
of Chimborazo in Ecuador. Anna Atkins was a botanist and the first
female photographer. She used a cyanotype process, placing algae
on paper treated with ferric ammonium citrate and citrate ferricyanide,
exposed to sunlight, then washed in water, turning uncovered areas
of the paper a velvety blue laced with white filigreed silhouettes
of what had once lain there, heavy and still in the warmth of the sun.
At 32 degrees, her cyanotypes are somewhere between the skies
of the Caribbean and the ones at Teide. In the article on apophenia,
which I read after the chapter on a nineteenth-century physicist
talking himself into unseen worlds ordered by a thermodynamic

God, I found an explanation for why it always seems I have
walked into a library and been handed just the book I needed.
A pale sky coming to my senses, I can see there is no book
that is not a book I need. They're like light on the water, the way
Anna lays them on the page after page—*Cystoceira granulata,*
Polysiphonia violacea, Chordaria flagelliformis. It feels like she's touching
my cheek across two hundred years, a little brush of seaweed
that before I thought was the sensation of the one I cannot be with
thinking of me, but was actually me thinking of what I thought
was him through those invisible inventions, those particles some
scientists called demons, like a joke or an attempt to keep believing.
With apophenia it's hard to know where you are supposed to stop.
I don't think you are supposed to stop. That he doesn't love me
is just another fiber to weave. Though it be a mania, a symptom
of insanity, though maybe no one will follow me down through
the center of this knot. A doctor who shared the same room with me
and the same moment in time said so generously that apophenia
doesn't necessarily mean you're going crazy. "Our relentless
detection of patterns is a defense mechanism, instinct. It is a great
challenge, learning to bear incoherence." When William Barrett was
watching a candle-blossom of flame twitch to every sound,
like a nervous and sensitive person, he wondered why some of us
might not be analogous to such flames, attuned to vibrations
beyond our senses. I feel it like it must be true: Alexander
and Anna found each other in time, on a cliff overlooking gardens
of the sea and are kissing like it's the end of the world. Can you
feel how his lips brush against yours? How hers do? How
there's nothing you can see but the blank page of that deepest blue
they would have found at Chimborazo if they hadn't run out of air
before reaching the summit and been forced to turn back?

Clear and Direct Discourse

I thought here and there throughout the day
about how we'd have sex when night came
and then, after I pulled off both our glasses
and pressed you against the wall, what I got
was a whole lot of distracted clumsiness
and the expectation I would keep on providing
this astonishing show of being an entirely
different woman from the one I am. Sometimes
it really is too many miles, so I get you done
and then find my T-shirt and underwear,
and roll over hoping maybe you can find
a way to me, but not hoping nearly as much
as I did all day. This is why I lost interest
in the first place. It's too hard to want and fail,
to feel the rough edges of the person
you're supposed to be trying to be when
you're trying to figure out how to be yourself
thrilling electric in response to you over there,
feeling so bad, so emasculated, so sorry to be
this kind of failing man, when all I had to do
was say, vis-à-vis the marriage counselor's
suggestion, what I want when I want it.
I did not want to say the word "lube." I wanted
to hint at it, because "lube" is gross, as a word,
as a product, that I need it, that I want it.
I know I'm supposed to be more sex-positive,
GGG, blah blah blah, but I'm just not. I'm
just myself, which is to say, of course I could
climb on top and make it happen. Of course
I know how to make you feel better. When you
miss the past of us, is that what you're missing?
Did you know it only works if I make myself
mean it? I have to mean it that it's more

important for you to feel okay than it is for me
to feel peeved about the disconnect during
and the widening mouth after of you trying
to touch me this way and trying to touch me
that way and none of it what I want. It's a spell
and you're sad because you didn't even know
there was a spell, much less why I won't do it
now. Let's try something new I like to call
"What Is Real." It goes like this: Lover,
you're being limp-wristed and whiny and I don't
feel like being a sexed-up vixen on top.
The handbook to save our marriage says
I'm supposed to find a way to remember
I'm an animal. I just want to find a way to forget
I'm alive. Maybe that's even more fucked up.
Maybe I'll turn out to be a sex-positive animal
reincarnated on the other side. Who knows?
Just because I read the book doesn't mean I know
the answers. And anyway, this is how it's been
as long as I've known you. I do all my homework,
you didn't even know there was homework.
Lover, you get an F. It was an F. It just was.
Of course you have potential. You've had
potential for as long as I've known you. I don't
know if I have potential. No one ever said that
to me. They assessed the work I handed in
on time and according to the directions.
I could be a gold star gliding my exceptional
work ethic across the top of your body,
but I'm old now and before I die I'd like to
know how it feels to be nothing but untapped
potential. I know it's petty, it's mean, it's against
the rules, but tonight I'm rolling over. I'm going
to sleep angry, just to see what that feels like.
I'll tell you what it feels like. It feels real.

A Great Place to Raise Children

I hardly feel anything these days beyond the boredom
that makes it seem only a promotion with a raise could
give a thrill now. I mean there is no such thing as sky
or I mean I don't know how to turn myself back on.
I mean I drink as much as is reasonable and it does
make things a little more rosy-fingered than they were
when I woke up in this pale pink dress of a gray morning's
wheat field. Stillness, of course, has its Andrew Wyeth
retrospectives to recommend it, but I'm in my J. M. W.
Turner and the tornadic sky phase. I spent yesterday
in the company of small children. Small children make
my small daughter so happy. If I look at her sky I can
be a little kite on the wind about it too, but then
her very annoying buddy is in what his mother calls
"a Band-Aid phase," where sometimes, despite how
there is no injury and no blood, he decides he needs
a Band-Aid and wails in a way that wrecks the air
down to the very molecules until someone runs out
to the minivan to raid the first-aid kit and you better
hope there is a Pokémon on that unearthed Band-Aid
or there will be no end. I tried to keep my refusal
and disdain of this getting of Band-Aids to myself,
because I know it only seems I can parse the difference
between loving kindness and a spoiled brat. Can you
believe the whole point of orgasms is this? From
the nervous thrill of a kegger on East Campus to
the feathery glitter of this pair of new earrings, it's all
for the creation of a snot-faced wailing four-year-old
in the ball pit at Going Bonkers? When I have a great
orgasm the sky turns into Turner's portrait of Parliament
on fire. When I just have an orgasm, I remember
he chose the brightest paints he could find and didn't care

that they start to fade the moment you brush them on.
Dealers and critics complained, but he wasn't concerned
about museums a hundred years out, so now you must
try to imagine the riot of storm through the almost
invisible serenity of pastels under glass. I don't know
what the point is. Perhaps the point is drunk? Or high?
Or—otherwise? Ruskin was the nineteenth-century
art critic who loved how Turner blew up the blue sky.
To paraphrase his masterpiece, *Modern Painters*, Vol. 1:
If you must prefer to savor a blue sky, at least notice
there is no monochrome of blue; the painters lie to you.
Ruskin hates lies. He hates the lie of order, the lie
of geometry, the lie of serenity. Does the great Turner
make you feel a chaos the chest of your eye can't contain?
Well, you wouldn't do well to stare directly into the sun
either. Well, you know there is an endless sea of sugarcane
fields on the empire's other horizon. Well, you know
there are fires burning a constellation of islands across
that long night of the Atlantic. A still life is just a portrait
of things a rich man owns coupled up with a lie of meaning.
All those fine landscapes foregrounded with English
gardens and a well-dressed couple on a park bench
are commissioned portraits too of the land the commissioner
calls his own. How is it, Turner asks with each crimson
stroke, that we even abide such pictures, much less pay
to hang them on a wall and gaze in satisfaction at how we own
them? We'd have to have no idea what a feeling was to take
such pleasure. We'd have to think we exist for the sake
of something else altogether. Well, I have a feeling, I have
an idea, I know a pleasure. Fuck the sky, I say. Burn it down.

Letter Home

I've been leaving and I'm not done leaving yet. I pretended
for almost ten years that I was a farmer's wife and I liked
sinking into seventeen acres. I tried to believe I could
make a life out of watching what those grasses in the meadow
would do next if we just kept not mowing them down.
I tried to distract myself with novelties like goats and eggs
and flowers it's surprising you can eat and other flowers
it's surprising you can use for an abortion or aspirin.
I tried to believe I could stay for a baby, so I had a baby,
but babies need you to pretend you're all the way home
and you always will be. They need you to say about 2000 words
an hour and smile at them often, the parenting book experts
told me in the quiet empty of that home two hours from anybody
who likes me, or else they won't learn to talk or process
emotion in a developmentally appropriate way and they too
will end up people who often stare with no emotion at a wall
hours away from anyone who likes them. I don't ever go
in the bathroom and cry, but I think about how I could
if I really had to and that takes the edge off. My husband
is so sweet, cutting onions as he says, "Let's just move
to California. Or let's just move to Ohio. Or Spokane.
Let's pack the car for Spokane." He's trying to make up for
a time when he didn't love me this much, but it's enough
and it's made up. I'm just afraid we'll get wherever and wherever
will be here again. "I don't think it will work," I say. "Of course
it won't work," he says. "You're trying to outrun death.
But the ocean, the boxes, the little fears of starting, it will be
years before you feel it again." He means home's hot breath
on the back of our necks. "This is what people do?" I ask,
wiping my eye quick, so our five-year-old, skipping through
the kitchen doesn't see. "It's one of the things they do," he says.
And then while the little she is stuffing a cracker in her mouth,

he passes behind her head so she can't see him as he says,
"There's also this," and holds his finger to his temple as he
fires his thumb. I'm laughing with my head on the table
so she can't see I'm crying that he knows so much.

Hexagenia Limbata

This bug with a needle out the back that might be
its stinger or a body's length of genital or just
the endlessness of an unlikely thorax has translucent
black-leaded wings and picks its way across my table
in this bar, lifting its skinny ass up and down in a way
you'd have to agree is sexy. What shall we call it?
A man I know who likes to read archaic Latin
just came in and didn't recognize me, so I watched
him walk away in his humble slouch of cargo shorts
and bald head, a little overweight, thinking to myself
that if he were to sit down next to me and read
this passage or that from some very old tract
on Roman property law for no other reason than
he likes what language can do, I would kiss him
up and down his throat and into his mouth, one
sentence at a time. Among other reasons, to help
me forget how earlier today I read the transcripts
of that poor girl's testimony against a Harvard-bound
ambassador's son and how she just couldn't believe
what was happening to her was happening to her,
so she was quiet when he did it, and tried for two days
after to believe she had asked for it and there was
nothing to report. Because how do we live in the world
if it wasn't our fault? Easier if we should have just
said or done something different. I'll walk home
alone and tipsy tonight, as my friend who never
even got to testify did, because it's a great pleasure
to be by yourself, drunk with the night. Though
it's hard not to think about how she was grabbed
by the throat under just so many stars. She was afraid
and she wanted to get away, so she offered to blow
him instead, because, she said later, we've all done

things we didn't feel like doing just to get it over with.
I'll remember how I tried to explain this to my dad
once at the end of a long drive. That I too really love
to walk home alone in the dark, but he didn't get it.
Words never seem to live up to the promise they make us.
Why would I want to do something so stupidly
dangerous? he asks. Another night we were talking
about politics and transvaginal ultrasounds and I said
nonchalantly that I've had six of them because once
you've had six you can't help but be nonchalant
about it. He was shocked so I explained it was
the miscarriage and the retained placenta. They call
the thing a wand, but it looks just like a dildo
and the nurse puts a condom on it for hygiene
and practicality. "No need to reinvent the wheel,"
she jokes as she rolls the latex down in front of you.
But since language can't reinvent what happens
to you, it still feels really screwed-up to lie on a table
with a lube-soaked, condom-covered dildo in your body
watching the movie it projects onto a flat-screen TV
of your larger-than-life dead baby who isn't really a baby
or other times it's just the emptiness inside yourself
the doctor is pointing at. There's language again,
twisting what is into what isn't. It was a baby to me—
I don't expect it to have been to you. This time
my dad is wiping his eyes, I can't believe it,
but he is. Maybe because, and this hadn't occurred
to me before, but maybe he loved that child
who never was and maybe because he loves me too.
My stranger with his Latin writes about linguistics
and philology and charmed me once by saying
he likes the puzzle words make, how he can
take them apart and apart and apart and then
reassemble them into a language more familiar
while he drinks alone at this bar in this private life

of his with no woman and no man. All the while
that strange, unknown insect with a body like lace
has been crawling along my arm. I didn't notice.
Does it even have a mouth at this stage in its life?

The New Elements

Elements can be named after a scientist,
a mineral, a place or a country, a property,
or a mythological concept. The four new
elements, all of which are synthetic,
were discovered by slamming lighter nuclei
into each other and tracking the resulting
decay of the radioactive superheavies.
I don't know about you, but I'm tired
of making things out of other things.
I came out to this bar to read the news
in the company of people falling in love
for only the second or third time. Like
other superheavies that populate the end
of the periodic table, the new ones exist
for only fractions of a second before
dissolving into more familiar atomic particles.
Is it true that I'm here hoping a stranger
might take me home? Of course it is.

Rue

"Let's try again," he says.

I could, but I wear this pressed flower around my neck, as all the girls once wore a charm, and it will not let me believe never anymore a promise.

I could, but the archangel gave Adam yellow blossoms of rue that he might have clear sight. And Eve, merciful midwife that she was, snuck her own bouquet.

I could, but it is rue in Saint Hildegard's curious book of visions and apocalypses that is the remedy for melancholy.

I could, but rue is bitter, hence regret, and rue is the antidote to plague, hence the fair maidens.

I could, but the basilisk's breath, which causes plants to wilt and stones to crack, has no effect on rue.

But the weasels who hunt the snakes first gorge themselves on rue, the herb of grace, and grave robbers in shackles traded the secret recipe to the Vinegar of the Four Thieves for their freedom.

Rosemary, sage, lavender, rue, wormwood, meadowsweet, cloves, campanula roots, two ounces of angelica, three pints of strong white vinegar, horehound, and large measures of camphor protects the wearer against pestilence and plague.

I could, but could you tell me the name of even one such star that constellates the ocean of these endless brown fields?

"Our Savior rebuked the Pharisees their superstition in paying tithes in rue."

The priests used rue to see the witches and the witches used rue to see the priests.

Da Vinci and Michelangelo both took rue to preserve their vision and keep it sharp.

I could, but blind men can't paint virgins.

I could, but when I wanted to, you were nowhere to be found.

I could, but I like you better when I hardly recognize you this way.

I could, but for how rue loves the rocky, sandy soil. But for how it makes a yellow meadow of this fall-down stone wall.

I could, but I don't even think I could.

I could, but I don't think I will.

A Lee Bontecou Retrospective

To look at Lee Bontecou's sculptural amalgamations
of so much paint is to remember how disordered
a brain must be to look at a hole or a circle or a bulge
of a hypothetical pupil and not immediately think
of a human face. One face after another has done
experiments on us to confirm we can't help
but see ourselves reflected in wall outlets,
sink faucets, the rear bumper of a 1997 Sedan.
Lee Bontecou puts her not-eyes everywhere
and after a while it felt like I went to outer space
where every star is an eye orbited by smaller eyes
inside of which live in blinking interdependence
epochs upon lineages of more microscopically far-off
eyes. And after that while it felt like my body
was an expression of the laws of physics
as opposed to a function. As in, I'm floating
through the vacuum of it all with my eyes closed.

A brain must be at least a little disordered not to
look at a sideways eye careening through the galaxy
and think of a vagina, though as Lee Bontecou
gets older the eyes increasingly appear inside
of complicated sailboat apparatuses, the canvas
triangles pointing in conflicting directions. Sometimes
I worry about massive political systems. Sometimes
I worry about my private relationships. Sometimes
I feel like I am the eye inside the boat and saying
something will make a difference. Other times
it is clear an eye has no mouth, no hand, no keel.

Lee Bontecou has so many combinations—
sails on the bottom, sails at perpendicular

angles, sails for eyelashes. I am not an eye,
I am a boat. I am not a boat, I am a barrel
stitched out of animal skins and left
on my side to gaze through the next 10,000
years of vessels on the water brushing
against this perimeter of air. I don't like it
down here in this burlap sack of body,
but I do like it. I am and am not the deer
I roused from the thicket of thorns.

Her life went on a long time and the eyes
went on procreating like there was this one
great God asleep inside the old hill of himself
thinking into being all these blinks of eyeballs
roving their pupils floating over the sails
of countryside. Only a disordered brain
will fail to notice how much an eye looks
like a UFO. In *Optics* Aristotle said yellow
and gray make blue. Was he disordered to see it
that way or am I disordered to say I see
what he means? Turn the page and he'll say
the eye is the beginning of knowing.

Sometimes I can't tell if I'm looking at a painting
or if Lee Bontecou killed one of those giant sloths
that used to eat the tops of pine trees. I've been
having drinks with a man who is kinder and makes
more sense now that he's living with a different heart
than the one he started with. It seems a lot like
when you have a C-section and they actually take
all of your organs out and put them on the table
for a while, then put them all back in less
an extraneous baby or two. And afterwards
you have these dreams where you are holding
a squishy sort of apple saying, "Holy shit,

what part of me *is* that?" Any of these organs
could fit inside one of the eye caves Lee Bontecou
makes that are beautiful, once you've seen enough
of them to get your algorithms of beauty reset.

Once it seemed like I had all of these feelings
and also none of them. It seemed like it would
be so easy to know which if I weren't stuck
inside this spaceship with its bad glaucoma
of a cracked windshield. But now I have gone
to outer space with Lee Bontecou's eyes, which are
not eyes, and her gaze, which shows how you don't
have to keep being human if you don't want to.

Regarding Silphium, the Birth Control of the Roman Empire for 600 Years, Extincted by Careless Land Management in the Year 200 A.D.

When I was just about done being married
and he was a blossomed-out nerve of seeing
himself through the ugly eyes of how I had
come to see him and myself for letting
our lives get so Tupperware-fur-molded,
for thinking I could lace and pinprick it back
with just the right delicacy, when a good
punch in the face was what a mess this bad
required. (I know, you're thinking a punch
in the face is never the answer, but that's
the lace talking.) When I was just about done
with the lace-throated maybe-violence,
our daughter, who is five, told me how
he broke—she didn't say he broke, she said
he got really worked up—driving past
all the protesters outside Planned Parenthood
on Providence Ave., from which the university
medical school had just withdrawn funding
and also the option for residents to do
training there, how he took a hard left
into the parking lot and with our daughter
by the hand marched in with an urgency
that made the young man working the desk
say, "Sir?" with some alarm. He took a breath
to be more steady and said, "I'm so sorry
about all of this—all of that out there—
and I just thought I'd make a donation"
as he pulled all the money from his wallet,
some of it crumpled, a mixture of 5s and 1s

and pushed it across the counter, our daughter
watching and looking around the room,
studying the faces of timid and nervous
young women, I imagine, in those plastic
chairs I remember from when I once sat
in this exact waiting room myself, so many
years ago, feeling embarrassed and ashamed
because it seemed that's what I was supposed
to feel, though if I could have felt my way
beyond "supposed to" back then to my
actual self, I would have known I didn't feel
sorry at all, only annoyed by the tedium
of appointments, the practical necessity
of that clean smell, the chilly dustless air
of a building with nothing soft except
the aspect of the resident, who is the only
doctor I have ever had who joked as she
put her gloved hand in my body. "I guess this
is the most awkward thing you'll do today,
huh?" It was funny and made me feel like
we'd been friends a long time. My husband,
who is still my husband after all, knew
that story and I guess he wanted our daughter
to somehow know it too. "Sometimes
you'll feel very alone," I tell her on a day
when I find her pressing her face against
the window, watching the children next door
play in the grass, wiping tears from her face
as fast as they fall. "Other times you'll be
so wonderfully surprised by the strange bridges
people manage to build out to you when
you never would have expected they could."

The Unicorn Tapestries

In the Renaissance there were the masters who could do skies—
their parting of clouds, their terrifying wings of an angel
were the feathered breaths of a reflected light. They had
apprentices to do the foxes and rabbits, gerbils and fawns
gathering in the grass around the saint's naked feet.
In the ICU I marveled at his mouth, without dentures
or muscles, how everyone who dies opens their mouth this way.
Everyone who dies this way, it seems, does it on the edge
of morning, perhaps so that after we can walk out
into the beginning of a day with his watch in a pocket
dragging heavy in a way he is not. Or maybe he is just so heavy.
On the lawn of the hospital come these fat rabbits
to graze and roll on their backs and stretch to scratch themselves.
To make you imagine their purring. What had been raccoons rattling
the purple end of night are now the School Sisters of Notre Dame,
some still in wimples, all in skirts to the knee, dark nylons,
and orthopedic shoes, pushing walkers or holding each other
by the elbow on the way to chapel. He shared their nursing home—
it was an endless source of amusement to him to tell
the other lays in residence, "My last home should be a convent,
my first had eleven sisters!" They would know soon
and cry a little for him, as they do for someone every morning
of their lives in this assisted-living wing tucked under
the hospital's shadow. Two floors above us is the resident
who, in the moment of crisis, put in the tube and the needle
and the smaller one and the other one, who waited to see
all the lines beep their slow rhythm and then called the people
who would have wanted to hold his hand when he was afraid
and she the only one there in the empty quiet of the graveyard shift.
Did she speak to him as she worked? I think she would have.
When we were ready to ask, she pulled out that huge tube
from his throat. He didn't even cough. You can almost see her

through the glass, whited light by morning. She's drawing out
the rest of her work, the catheter and the IV and the little box
around his finger. She's lifting the weight of him with the corners
of a blanket, first his head, then his feet. She is the one
who will pull up the sheet. I read her name on her ID badge
and for a moment I knew it, but forgot, even though I could tell
it was a name I would always want to remember, the name
of this most cherished of strangers from a morning
when I cherished everyone I ever knew or didn't, when I wanted
to hold the hand of the person who dappled in the tufts
of violets and dandelions, these rabbits that are such plump bodies—
you have to find a way to paint their heft, to show how there is
weight in there that swallows the light not to reflect it right back.

This Is Your Mother Calling

Having a baby is awesome, I definitely recommend it,
in the same way I encourage you to go to the hospice
wing and hold what part of your father's body you can
reach through the tubing as he makes those rough last
breaths. Hemorrhaging in the bathroom of your workplace
is another good revelation, as is the hand of the pale-faced
boss who walks you unsteady out to the waiting car
of the colleague from the cubicle over who drives you
to the emergency room saying gently, "You'll be alright,
you really will." You should let yourself love that kid
who shows up in your class or courtroom or church
or wherever you are, love him like a son, even though
you know he is going to end up in jail or suicide. And
when he's looking for someone to turn unpredictable
and dangerous on, you may as well raise your hand
for that too. For God's sake, whatever you do, don't
skip the affair. Or the drugs. Don't forget to drink
even after you know you should stop. The hardest part
is calling that best friend from high school to make
a lunch date. What room could she have in her life
for the messy-haired notebooks of you after so many
years? What could you tell her that will make her glad
she loaded up the car seats of her later-life miracles
for this coffee over the sounds of these crying children?
But do it anyway and slip a cookie to the older one
who misses his mother, just lost her to the red-faced
wails of that piglet in the baby carrier she makes those
beautiful smiles over. I don't recommend telling him
how much he looks like your own beloved child,
but I do suggest telling him the truth—"Mothers
are very tired, dear, and all of their smiles are the fake
smiles of doing what's necessary to make it through

these years of so much nothing happening but happy
little days of health, steady income, home ownership,
which some day sooner than we think we'll say we miss."
After you lose your job, I recommend losing the rest of it
too—the good manners, the polite tongue, the casual
slacks, that old water heater rusting a hissing steam
of men in coveralls estimating what you really need
as the chimney collapses in a little brick tumble
of rotted-out tuck pointing. The doctors will recommend
the chemo, a finger's width of a tube pouring a cold
clear drip into the big vein of your forearm. After,
whether you'd do it all again, that's not for me to say,
but if it were, I'd go for the roachy one-bedroom
of what was it all for anyway? You can keep a little
of all that old mercy, but at least break a lamp before
you say, "I understand your point of view." Hopefully
before, but maybe after that daughter or son of yours
will get the hang of pedaling a two-wheeler without you,
get going down the sidewalk so fast you can't even run
to keep up. I can't recommend it, but if it's going to
happen, you may as well know. When it does, I suggest
you sit down on the stoop of wherever your life is
and let yourself have a good cry. I recommend you go
ahead and light a cigarette if you're in the mood, even if
that big kid of yours sees you setting such a bad example.
A lucky child will see much worse before it's all done.

Pissy Bitch Middle-Aged Happy

I probably always loved nature
but came late to understanding it
or maybe that's how it is for everybody.
By the time you know you don't want
to eat the serviceberries lining the trail
unless things have gotten truly dire
you might be feeling pretty dire.
The skin on the whole bottom half
of my face is so loose now I feel it
sort of flopping around down there.
I chew a little on the inside part
sometimes when I'm concentrating
because I'm old and there's just so much
extraneous face of me down there
at the bottom half of my face.
If you asked, I'd describe myself
as looking a bit like a pissed-off possum.
Not that I'm complaining. It's a great face,
relatively speaking, and anyway I hardly
ever have to look at it. I use it for staring
at these pines that tree their way down
to that stretch of water in an interlocking
pattern of thinner and fatter trunks
weaving under and over the crinkles
of my birch-bark eyes. I've lived long
enough now to know when a hillside
was clear-cut and then replanted
in a single afternoon as opposed to left
alone for enough years that the forest
happened without intention or just
an infinite number of individual intentions,
some of which were choked out or eaten

and others compromised by a fast-growing
shade, but glad enough to be even sideways
and hard-scrabbled in their reaching,
considering the alternatives. Although
not every juniper bush can be a glass-half-full
kind of evergreen. For me, for instance,
life has turned out pretty good,
and still I say, "Fuck you, Douglas fir,
firm and lush and tall, for taking up so much
of my sky." And then I smile to myself,
because it's funny to be so petty
inside a face with all this skin, enough
to fill a room if I were to stretch it out.

The Real Thing

Sir John Mandeville, the great explorer and liar,
claimed, "there grows a kind of fruit as big
as a gourd, and when it is ripe men open it
and find inside an animal of flesh and blood
and bone, like a little lamb without wool."
He called this the Vegetable Lamb of Tartary.

I first learned of it from a very old hippie
who was feeling lonesome one lavender
night of a misty joint for the lambskin
condoms of his soft-hearted youth. And also,
most likely, for a time when women in their
twenties heard such a line with more thrill
and less derision. A time when he didn't
get on a bicycle and think about his prostate,
get on a woman and think about his grave.

When Trojan brought them back as a mass
market consumable experiment in nostalgia
and the idea of the natural, my husband,
who would prefer to have another child
truth be told, bought a box for us to try.

After, we assessed. I've had better sex, but
there was a sort of hallucinatory flower
opening at the end, so that's something.

I've been reading about hallucinatory flowers
lately, particularly the ones used by medieval
midwives to induce abortion. This because
I like irony, I like control, and I like to see
a woman flipping the patriarchy the bird.

In my daily life though I stick with condoms,
because once the roots are in you, it's no mean
feat to get them out. It will feel like and be
a measure of poison. I think of the women
who once did the washing at the river with
a pair of stones and the meat of their arms.
I admire, but would not care to be, them.

When I took the little hormone pills, I always
worried I wasn't smelling things—pheromones
of men, lilacs, coffee, puddles around the gas
station—as they were meant to be smelled.
Meant to be, I'm learning, is a dangerous notion.

Goethe said there was meant to be an Urpflanze,
an archetypal plant and prototype containing all
plants past and future. He could draw it, but
after many years of travel and searching had to
conclude there is, nevertheless, no such thing.

After equally many years, I'm starting to worry
that I am missing the point of my life. Was I
meant to be the ovary of a green calyx always
getting fatter? How will I think when I die?
I worry there can be nothing worse than realizing
your life wasn't what it was meant to be.

The Vegetable Lamb of Tartary, Mandeville reports,
grazed the leaves of its mother until its umbilical
vine dropped off. Then it became a lamb like any
other, with meat for slaughter and skin that is
said to feel as translucently delicate as a petal.

Is a petal meant to chafe?

I told my husband sometimes there's great
and sometimes there's good enough.
He said from his point of view there wasn't
really much difference and what difference
there was wasn't an improvement so much
as a variation. So we went to sleep, content
enough, perhaps content as we were meant
to be, perhaps just shades of that.

Acknowledgments

Thanks to the editors who first published these poems:

32 Poems: "Letter Home" and "The Petty Politics of the Thing";

The Account: "Queen of Barren, Queen of Mean, Queen of Laced with Ire," "Regarding Silphium, the Birth Control of the Roman Empire for 600 Years, Extincted by Careless Land Management in the Year 200 A.D." and "Pennyroyal";

The Collagist: "When We Dead Awaken";

Crazyhorse: "Poor Crow's Got Too Much Fight to Live";

FIELD: "It's Like She Loves Us and Like She Hates Us";

Florida Review: "I Want to Know You All";

Gettysburg Review: "The Real Thing";

Gulf Coast: "This Is Your Mother Calling";

Hobart: "*Paradise by the Dashboard Light*";

Horsethief: "You Get What You Get and You Don't Throw a Fit";

I-70 Review: "The New Elements" and "Pissy Bitch Middle-Aged Happy";

Origins: "I Want to Learn How" and "A Natural History of Columbine";

Poetry Daily: "The Real Thing";

Poetry International: "Clear and Direct Discourse," "I'll Show You Mine If You Show Me Yours," and "A Difficult Woman";

Rockhurst Review: "I'm Worried About You in the Only Language I Know How" and "A Lee Bontecou Retrospective";

Southern Indiana Review: "The Unicorn Tapestries";

Spoon River Review: "Things I Did Today Besides" and "Dear Reader, I've Been Preoccupied Lately by My Own Private Business";

Stirring: "Rue" and "The Bird of Paradise";

Third Coast: "The Threshold of the Unseen World";

Tin House: "Hexagenia Limbata";

Tongue: "A Great Place to Raise Children."

From the beginning this book was for Maya Jewell Zeller. It has turned out, to my happy surprise, to be for Brian Blair too. And of course, always, with love for Alice Nuernberger Blair.

Much gratitude to the friends who have been inspirations, readers, and editors along the way: Erin Adair-Hodges, Taneum Bambrick, Hadara Bar-Nadav, Jaswinder Bolina, Traci Brimhall, Darlena Ciraulo, Heidi Czerwiec, John Gallaher, V. V. Ganeshananthan, Jennifer Givhan, Rose Gubele, Jenny Hipscher, Ben Johnson, Douglas Kearney, Hyejung Kook, Ellie Kozlowski, Kate Lebo, Dana Levin, Sam Ligon, Adrian C. Louis, Galina Malikin, Polina Malikin, Jennifer Maritza McCauley, Marc McKee, Rachel Mehl, Erika Meitner, Wayne Miller, Jenny Molberg, Dinty W. Moore, Brett Ortler, Laura Read, J. Allyn Rosser, Kathryn Smith, Rich Smith, Paul Sturtz, Kim Todd, Nance Van Winckel, Ellen Welcker, and Ruth Williams.

Thank you to the National Endowment for the Arts for an individual artist grant that helped support the creation of these poems. And to the Spring Creek Project at the H. J. Andrews Experimental Forest for time and space to research.

I am grateful to many herbalists and historians whose writing and scholarship helped on my ethnobotanical expeditions into the archives. Especially Yota Batsaki, Surekha Davies, Pablo F. Gomez, Londa Schiebinger, Kim Todd, and Andrea Wulf. Sarah Nguyen's artist book *How Does Your Garden Grow?* introduced me to many of the abortifacients I've written about here and to the defiant beauty of the tall grass prairie where we found our lives. Hannah Hemmelgarn taught me how to find and know the plants in the Upper Hinkson, Lower Hinkson, and Grindstone watersheds. I am grateful to Emily Beck and Lois Hendrickson at the University of Minnesota Wangensteen Historical Library for inviting me to join the History of Herbalism reading group.

All of my appreciation to Peter Conners, Ron Martin-Dent, and Kelly Hatton at BOA for support, encouragement, and a poetry home.

About the Author

Kathryn Nuernberger's previous books of poetry are *The End of Pink* and *Rag & Bone*. Her collection of lyric essays is *Brief Interviews with the Romantic Past*. She has received research fellowships from the H. J. Andrews Experimental Forest, American Antiquarian Society and the Bakken Museum of Electricity in Life. Other awards include an NEA fellowship and the James Laughlin Prize from the Academy of American Poets. She teaches in the MFA Program at University of Minnesota and lives with her family in Minneapolis-St. Paul.

BOA Editions, Ltd. American Poets Continuum Series

Colophon

BOA Editions, Ltd., a not-for-profit publisher of poetry and other literary works, fosters readership and appreciation of contemporary literature. By identifying, cultivating, and publishing both new and established poets and selecting authors of unique literary talent, BOA brings high-quality literature to the public. Support for this effort comes from the sale of its publications, grant funding, and private donations.

The publication of this book is made possible, in part, by the special support of the following individuals:

Anonymous
Angela Bonazinga & Catherine Lewis
James Long Hale
Jack & Gail Langerak
Joe McElveney
Boo Poulin
Steven O. Russell & Phyllis Rifkin-Russell
William Waddell & Linda Rubel
Michael Waters & Mihaela Moscaliuc